T0402901

LET'S GET OUTDOORS!
Cross-country Skiing
by Christina Leaf
BLASTOFF! 2 READERS
BELLWETHER MEDIA • MINNEAPOLIS, MN

Blastoff! Readers are carefully developed by literacy experts to build reading stamina and move students toward fluency by combining standards-based content with developmentally appropriate text.

LEVELS

Level 1 provides the most support through repetition of high-frequency words, light text, predictable sentence patterns, and strong visual support.

Level 2 offers early readers a bit more challenge through varied sentences, increased text load, and text-supportive special features.

Level 3 advances early-fluent readers toward fluency through increased text load, less reliance on photos, advancing concepts, longer sentences, and more complex special features.

★ **Blastoff! Universe**

Reading Level

Grade K

Grades 1–3

Grade 4

This edition first published in 2024 by Bellwether Media, Inc.

Library of Congress Cataloging-in-Publication Data

Names: Leaf, Christina, author.
Title: Cross-country skiing / by Christina Leaf.
Description: Minneapolis, MN : Bellwether Media, 2024. | Series: Blastoff! readers. Let's get outdoors! | Includes bibliographical references and index. | Audience: Ages 5-8 | Audience: Grades 2-3 | Summary: "Relevant images match informative text in this introduction to cross-country skiing. Intended for students in kindergarten through third grade"– Provided by publisher.
Identifiers: LCCN 2023035157 (print) | LCCN 2023035158 (ebook) | ISBN 9798886877984 (library binding) | ISBN 9798886878929 (ebook)
Subjects: LCSH: Cross-country skiing–Juvenile literature.
Classification: LCC GV855.35 .L43 2024 (print) | LCC GV855.35 (ebook) | DDC 796.93/2–dc23/eng/20230804
LC record available at https://lccn.loc.gov/2023035157
LC ebook record available at https://lccn.loc.gov/2023035158

Editor: Elizabeth Neuenfeldt Series Design: Andrea Schneider Book Designer: Josh Brink

Printed in the United States of America, North Mankato, MN.

Table of Contents

What Is Cross-country Skiing?

Cross-country skiing
is a winter sport.
It is also called Nordic skiing.

People use skis and poles to **glide** over snow. They go far!

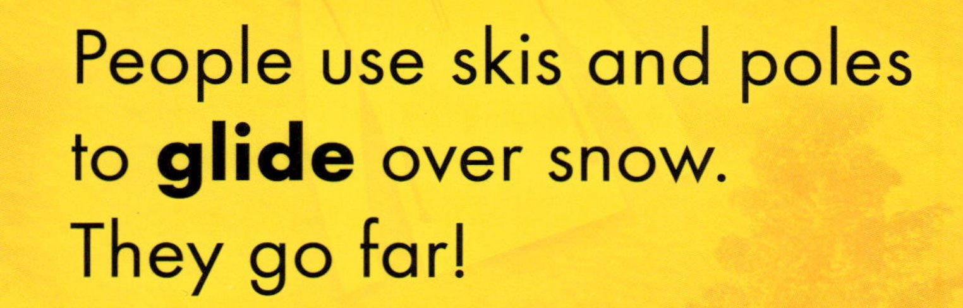

Most people ski on trails.
Trails may be flat or have hills.
Many go through woods.

Favorite Cross-country Skiing Spot

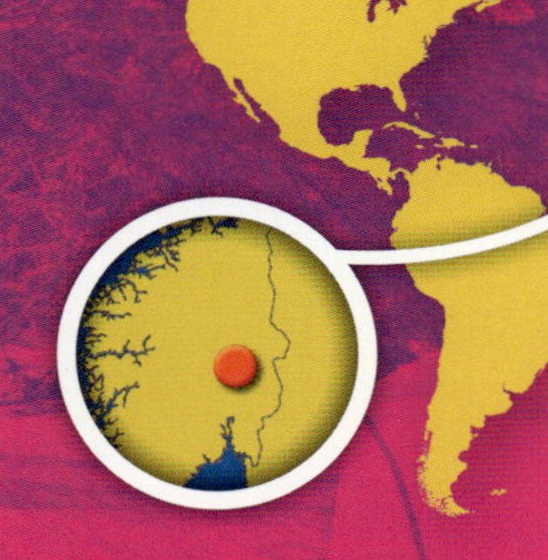

Sjusjøen, Norway

Claim to Fame

- around 218 miles (350 kilometers) of trails
- includes part of Norway's biggest race trail

ski race

Some skiers race. Others ski for fun. Skiers enjoy the beauty of winter!

Classic or Skate?

There are two ways
to cross-country ski.
Classic skiers ski in tracks.

Skate skiers ski on a flat **deck**.
Many places **groom** trails
for both kinds of skiing.

skate skier

classic skier
groomed
trail

Classic skiers push down on one leg. Then they kick back to glide forward.

They push on
the **opposite** pole
as they kick.

Skate skiers turn their feet out.
They kick one foot outward
to glide.

They push both poles at the same time.

Ways to Cross-country Ski

classic skiing

skate skiing

Cross-country Skiing Gear

Skate and classic skiers have different skis. Skate skis are smooth on the bottom.

Classic skis have rough or sticky patches. They **grip** the snow.

Special boots clip onto skis at the toe. Poles help skiers move and **balance**.

Jackets, hats, and gloves keep skiers warm.

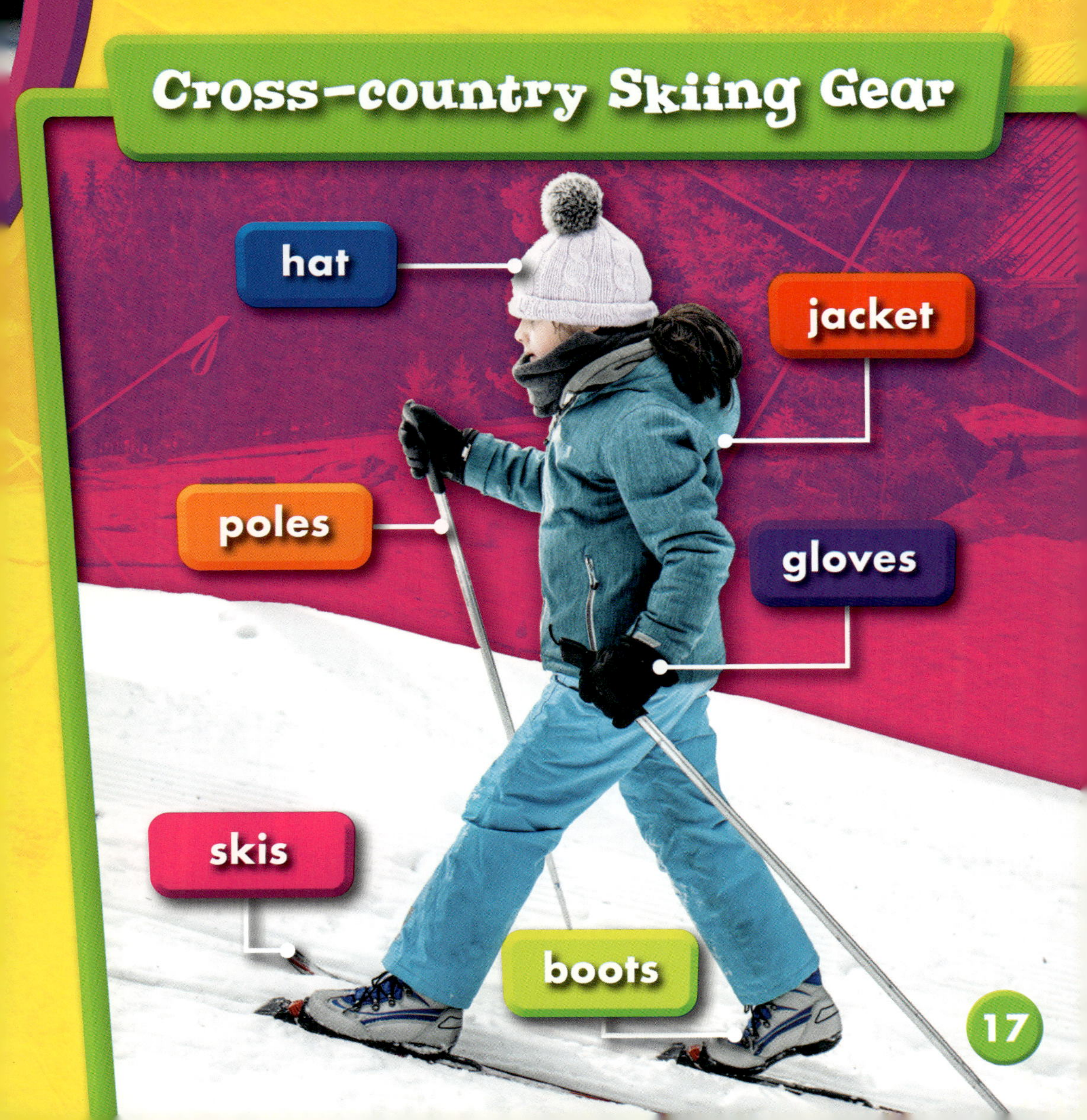

Cross-country Skiing Safety

Skiers may lose control on big hills. They can hurt themselves or others.

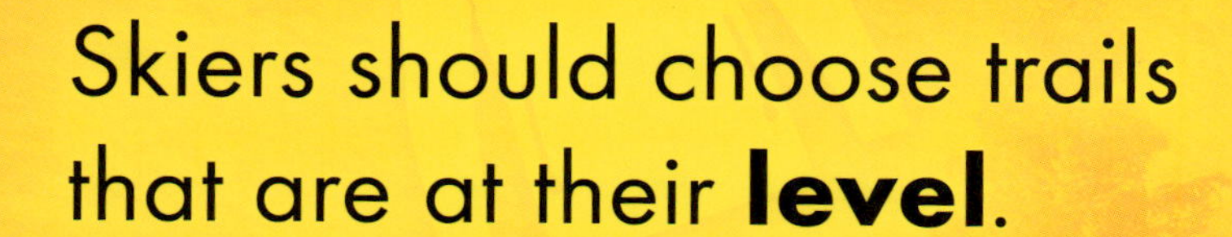

Skiers should choose trails that are at their **level**.

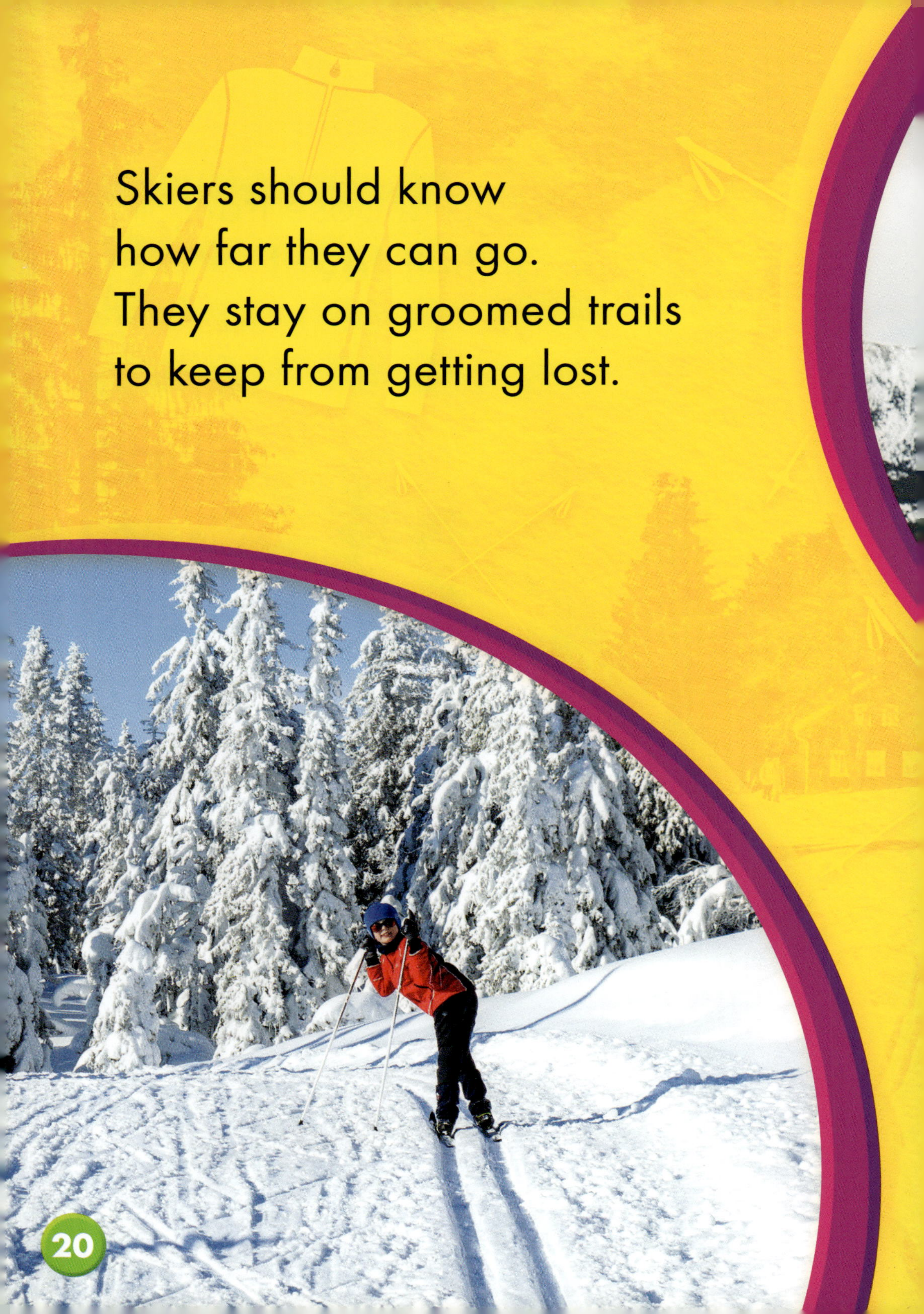

Skiers should know
how far they can go.
They stay on groomed trails
to keep from getting lost.

Cross-country skiing is
a great winter activity!

Glossary

balance—to stay steady and not fall

classic—related to a kind of cross-country skiing where skiers move in tracks

deck—a flat part of a cross-country ski trail where people can skate ski

glide—to move smoothly over something

grip—tightly hold onto something

groom—to make trails neat and ready for skiing

level—the amount of skill a person has

opposite—related to the other side

To Learn More

AT THE LIBRARY

Bode, Heather. *Go Skiing!* North Mankato, Minn.: Capstone Press, 2023.

Downs, Kieran. *Downhill Skiing.* Minneapolis, Minn.: Bellwether Media, 2024.

Waxman, Laura Hamilton. *Skiing.* Mankato, Minn.: Amicus High Interest, 2018.

ON THE WEB

FACTSURFER

Factsurfer.com gives you a safe, fun way to find more information.

1. Go to www.factsurfer.com.
2. Enter "cross-country skiing" into the search box and click 🔍.
3. Select your book cover to see a list of related content.

Index

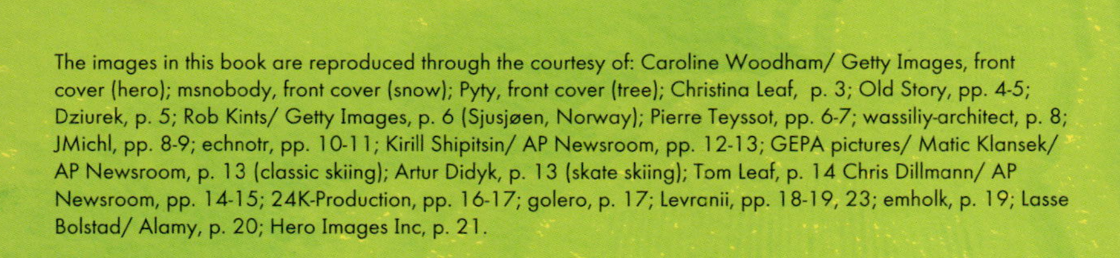

The images in this book are reproduced through the courtesy of: Caroline Woodham/ Getty Images, front cover (hero); msnobody, front cover (snow); Pyty, front cover (tree); Christina Leaf, p. 3; Old Story, pp. 4-5; Dziurek, p. 5; Rob Kints/ Getty Images, p. 6 (Sjusjøen, Norway); Pierre Teyssot, pp. 6-7; wassiliy-architect, p. 8; JMichl, pp. 8-9; echnotr, pp. 10-11; Kirill Shipitsin/ AP Newsroom, pp. 12-13; GEPA pictures/ Matic Klansek/ AP Newsroom, p. 13 (classic skiing); Artur Didyk, p. 13 (skate skiing); Tom Leaf, p. 14 Chris Dillmann/ AP Newsroom, pp. 14-15; 24K-Production, pp. 16-17; golero, p. 17; Levranii, pp. 18-19, 23; emholk, p. 19; Lasse Bolstad/ Alamy, p. 20; Hero Images Inc, p. 21.